New Zealand Cross-Stitch Embroidery Designs

Margaret Barrett

(Justine Jones)

David Bateman

Contents

ACKNOWLEDGEMENTS
Thanks to Amelia Bickerton, Dawn Johnston, Jennifer Jones, Tonia Muschamp, Yvonne Sturgess, Beverley Vining, Mary Frances Wells, Thelma Williamson and Mary Watkin.

First published in 1990 by
David Bateman Ltd
'Golden Heights', 32–34 View Road, Glenfield, Auckland 10, New Zealand

ISBN 1 86953 027 6

Photography by Karryn Muschamp
Typeset by Typocrafters Ltd, Auckland
Printed by Colorcraft, Hong Kong
Jacket design by Chris O'Brien

Introduction

Cross-stitch is a very traditional form of hand work and in our increasingly automated world there is something very peaceful about sitting down with a piece of cross-stitch while the world goes by.

The interest in cross-stitch has revived in recent years and it is now one of the most popular forms of needlework. One reason is its versatility — you can cross-stitch almost anything from a beautiful picture to a baby's feeder; from a cushion to a fine piece of table linen.

Cross-stitch also leaves lots of room for creativity in colour and design. As with many designs in this book you can change the colours, take out pieces and add ideas of your own. Never hesitate to do this as very often you will be delighted with the end result and the more you do it the more confidence it gives you to attempt your own designs.

Instructions

Working with a chart

Each square on a chart represents one cross-stitch on the fabric. If working in a linen or equivalent fabric your cross-stitch is always over 2 threads. If working on an Aida your cross-stitch represents one thread. Each symbol shown within the squares represents a different thread colour. The heavy black lines shown on a chart indicate back stitch. I have used back stitch to outline a particular part or to create a finer line than can be shown with cross-stitch.

To start your cross-stitch find the centre of your material by running a tacking thread lengthwise down your material and again crosswise. Each design has arrows marking the centre. Count from the centre to the highest point and commence work there, always working in the same direction. This is the golden rule of cross-stitch.

Do not knot your thread. To start and end off, run a thread under several stitches on the back to secure it.

When your embroidery is complete wash it gently by hand, using a mild soap. Rinse really well; do not wring. Place in a towel to remove excess moisture. Iron on a padded surface or a towel with a thick pile, making sure the embroidery is face down.

Equipment

Needles. A tapestry needle is always used for cross-stitch as it has a blunt end, which allows it to slip easily through the material you are using without splitting the thread.

Thread. I have used 6-stranded thread throughout this book and in most cases when working on the Jobelan I have used 2 of the 6 strands. If not sure on the count of your material always do a small 10×10-square of stitches to check how it covers the thread.

Fabric. There is a great choice of fabrics available today for cross-stitching. Choose the material most suited to your requirements, taking into consideration how the finished article is to be used, and your own eyesight — you want to enjoy your cross-stitch without having to strain to see it!

Scissors. A good pair of small sharp scissors is absolutely essential.

Hoop. A hoop for cross-stitch is purely optional. If you have been taught embroidery on a hoop you will find it much easier to use one. However always remember to remove your hoop when you have finished stitching for the day.

Detailed instructions

Diagram A. Sew cross-stitch from left to right. Sew all the under stitches first. Each of the under stitches goes diagonally over 2 threads from bottom left-hand corner. Sew the top stitches, on the way back, to complete the cross-stitch.

Diagram B. Cross-stitch sewn downwards: Finish each stitch before going on to the next, making sure that the over stitch lies in the same direction as in Diagram A. The wrong side of A and B should look like vertical stitching only.

Diagram C. Back stitch lines: Always work over 2 threads either horizontally or vertically, following the lines on the graph pattern and using the colour of that symbol.

Hibiscus

This is the single hibiscus and is a very popular garden shrub often growing to more than 2 metres high. The flower has 5 showy red petals and a long central column bearing a cluster of yellow stamens near the tip. The parent plant was originally a native of China and it has been propagated and developed all over the tropical and subtropical world. There are hundreds of varieties, all of great beauty.

This design lends itself to cross-stitch and is lovely worked on either a cream or white background. It is most attractive as a picture. The stamens are worked in straight stitches of 1 strand of gold.

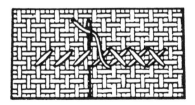
A

B

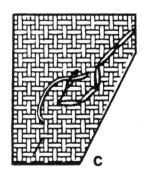
C

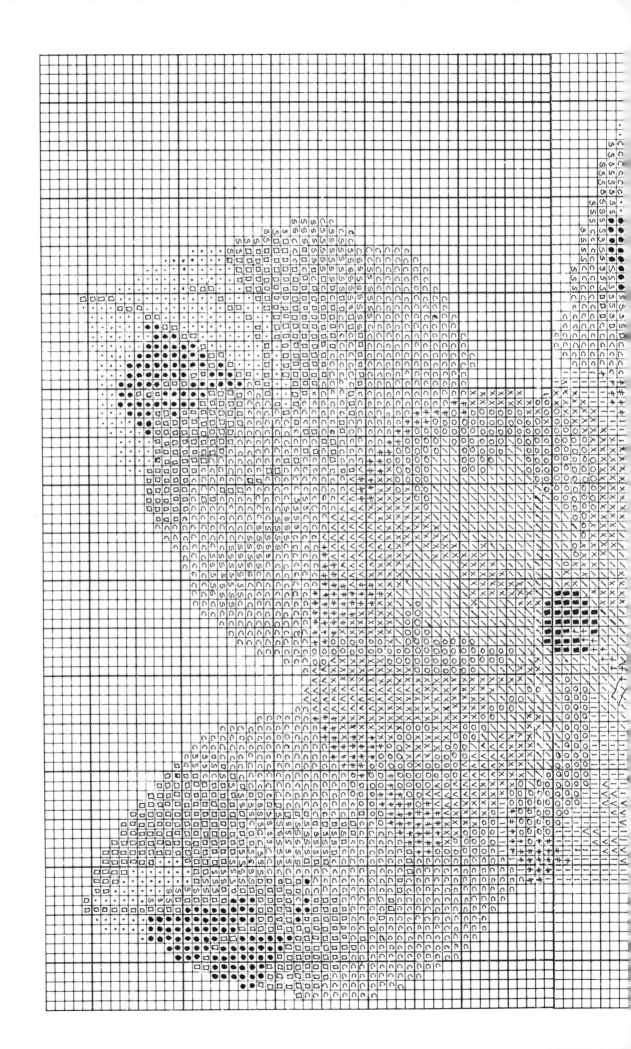

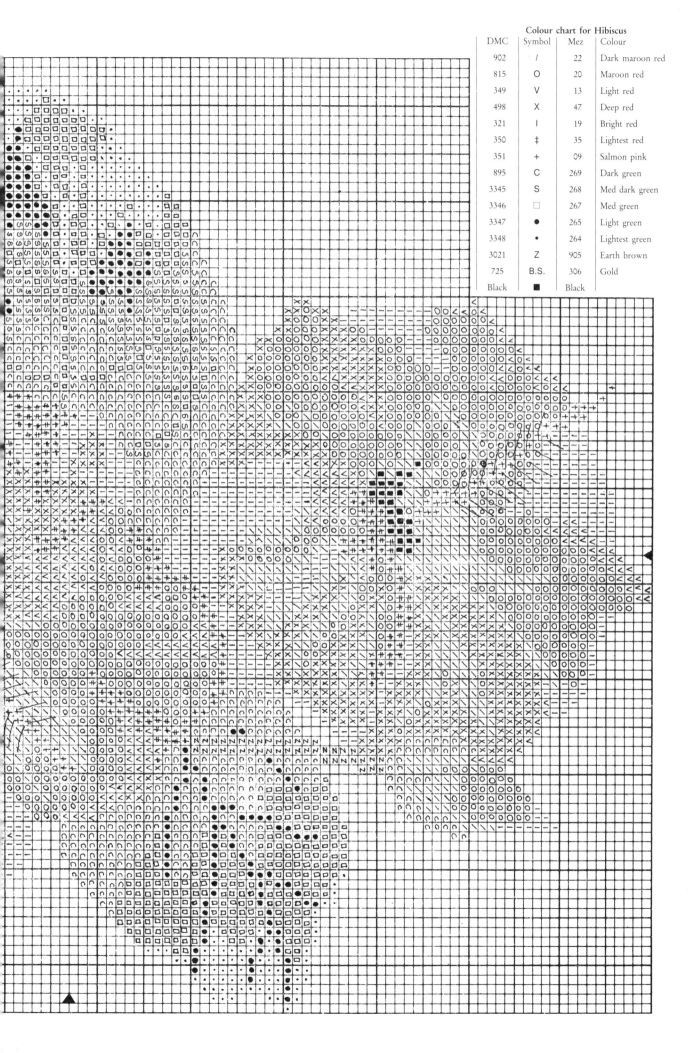

Colour chart for Hibiscus

DMC	Symbol	Mez	Colour
902	/	22	Dark maroon red
815	O	20	Maroon red
349	V	13	Light red
498	X	47	Deep red
321	I	19	Bright red
350	‡	35	Lightest red
351	+	09	Salmon pink
895	C	269	Dark green
3345	S	268	Med dark green
3346	□	267	Med green
3347	●	265	Light green
3348	·	264	Lightest green
3021	Z	905	Earth brown
725	B.S.	306	Gold
Black	■		Black

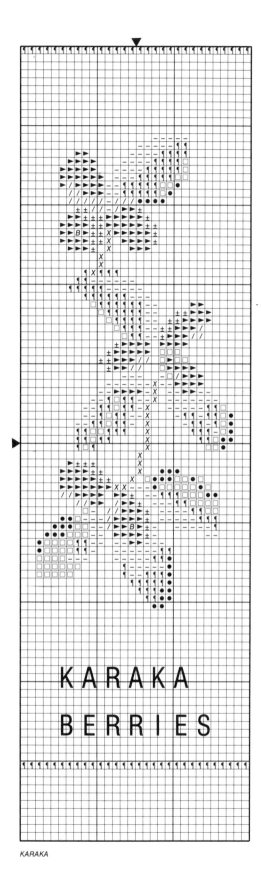

KARAKA

Karaka Berries

Stitch count 59×85

Karaka is the Maori name for this magnificent tree. The seeds were of great value to the Maori as a source of food. Karaka trees grow near the coast from North Cape down to Banks Peninsula. The leaves are dark, smooth and glossy and the berries ripen from green to yellow, then through to orange.

The small design can be used as a bookmark or small picture, and the writing can be worked in back stitch in dark green or black. The 2 models are worked on cream Jobelan.

Colour chart for Karaka Berries bookmark

DMC	Symbol	Anchor	Colour
935	–	269	Dark green
469	¶	267	Med green
3348	□	265	Light green
471	●	254	Med yellow green
3021	X	905	Earth brown
321	/	47	Bright red
606	►	335	Scarlet
971	±	316	Orange
Black	B	Black	

Colour chart for large Karaka Berries

DMC	Symbol	Anchor	Colour
839	X	905	Slate brown
869	O	889	Med brown
581	–	280	Muscat green
937	+	269	Moss green
469	●	267	Med moss green
319	P	245	Grass green
471	H	265	Light moss green
918	●	341	Terracotta
666	%	46	Scarlet
971	V	333	Orange
970	\	324	Light orange
973	∩	291	Yellow

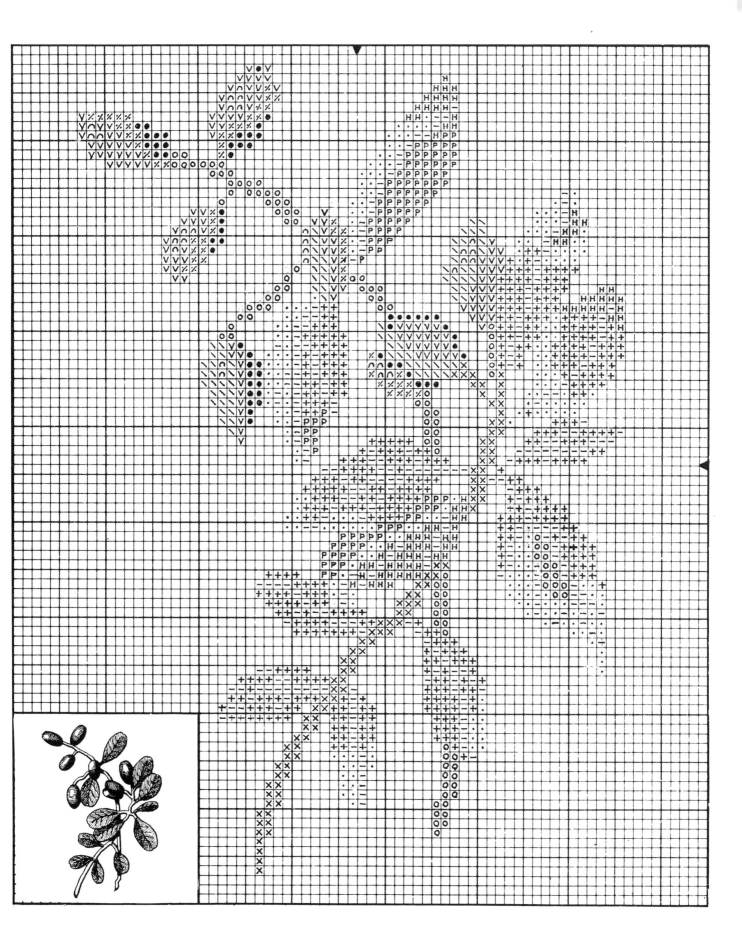

Kowhai

Stitch count 99 × 109

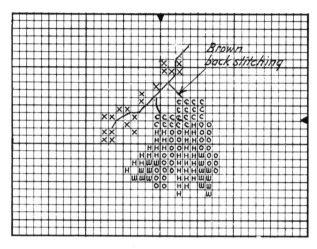

The model is stitched on grey Jobelan and the design was graphed for cross-stitch from a painting by Mary Watkin. It makes a lovely picture or can be made into a cushion or a table runner. The small kowhai is a very useful design for a card or very small frame or box.

Special stitching instructions: The stamen are worked in one long stitch of 905 (3021).

Kowhai is the Maori name for a tree that grows 12 metres high. It is a colourful tree producing quantities of nectar and attracts tuis, bellbirds and silvereyes. The tree loses its leaves in winter and the new leaves appear with the flowers in spring. It is found throughout New Zealand on the edges of forests and along the shores of lakes and inlets.

Colour chart for small Kowhai

DMC	Symbol	Anchor	Colour
581	C	280	Muscat green
726	H	295	Med yellow
307	O	290	Bright yellow
746	W	386	Cream
937	X	269	Dark moss green

Colour chart for large Kowhai

DMC	Symbol	Anchor	Colour
644	'	391	Fawn
640	–	903	Light earth brown
3021	×	905	Earth brown
781	O	309	Gold
725	|	306	Light gold
973	Z	290	Bright yellow
307	V	289	Yellow
745	•	300	Cream
935	H	269	Dark green
469	⌐	267	Med green
3348	∧	265	Light green

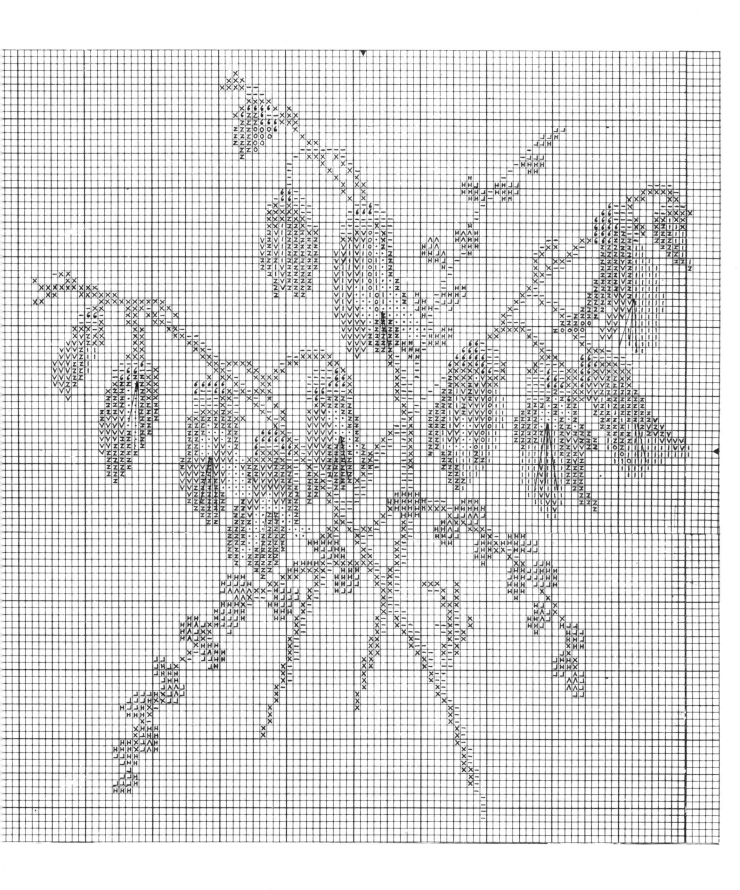

Mountain Buttercup

Stitch count 93 × 129

There are more than 40 varieties of mountain buttercup in the Ranunculus family. They grow along a large area of the Southern Alps and are also found in the Mt Ruapehu area. A fleshy rootstock penetrates the shingle and from this unlikely stony surface large flowers are raised.

The model is worked on grey Jobelan and this picture is one of a series of 3 paintings by Mary Watkin. It is most suitable as a picture or may be worked as a table runner or cushion.

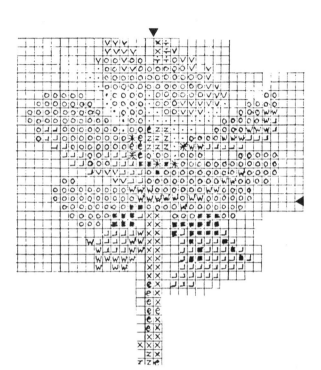

Colour chart for Mountain Buttercup

DMC	Symbol	Anchor	Colour
973	O	290	Bright yellow
307	V	289	Med yellow
727	•	293	Light yellow
935	Z	269	Dark green
937	X	268	Med green
469	–	267	Light green
3348	e	265	Lightest green
783	⌐	307	Gold
725	W	306	Light gold
640	✱	903	Light earth brown
472	\	253	Light yellow green
471	∧	254	Med yellow green
907	÷	255	Dark yellow green
934	C	862	Very dark green
781	■	309	Dark gold

Mt Cook lily

Stitch count 84×124

The Mt Cook lily is of the Ranunculus family, its latin name being *Ranunculus lyallii*, and is the largest and finest of its type in the world. The leaves are very large, reaching 30 centimetres across. The plant is found in subalpine areas from Marlborough south.

This design was taken from a painting by Mary Watkin and is most attractive worked in cross-stitch, but to be effective it should be worked on a colour other than white or cream. The model is worked on grey Jobelan. Either a soft green fawn or taupe would be most attractive as the background colour.

The design is suitable for a picture or cushion, or can be placed at either end of a table runner. One small flower can be taken out of the design for use on a card or small picture.

Colour chart for Mt Cook lily

DMC	Symbol	Anchor	Colour
White	•	White	
927	V	849	Blue grey
926	*	850	Dark blue grey
445	■	288	Yellow
934	Z	862	Very dark green
935	e	269	Dark green
906	X	256	Yellow green
907	●	255	Med yellow green
469			267	Med green
420	O	375	Tan brown
415	–	397	Pale grey

Cyclamen

Stitch count 122×112

The cyclamen is mainly used these days for ornamental purposes. Its dappled leaves and very elegantly shaped flowers make an attractive show. In days gone by the tuber was recommended by doctors as a strong purgative and was said to cure tumours, dropsy and other chronic diseases.

Its simple but elegant lines lend this plant to cross-stitch. This particular one I have worked in 5 shades of pink, but these colours can easily be changed to other toning shades to suit the area in which you may want to place the finished design.

The roots are worked in one thread and back stitched following the lines on the chart.

Colour chart for Cyclamen

DMC	Symbol	Mez	Colour
500	⊙	862	Darkest green
501	–	879	Dark green
502	¶	878	Med green
503	□	876	Light green
504	●	875	Lightest green
902	X	072	Deepest maroon
3685	E	071	Maroon
3686	S	077	Deep pink
3688	p	076	Med pink
3689	=	075	Med light pink
963	‡	073	Light pink
3371	C	382	Dark brown
3021	K	905	Earth brown
640	•	903	Light earth brown

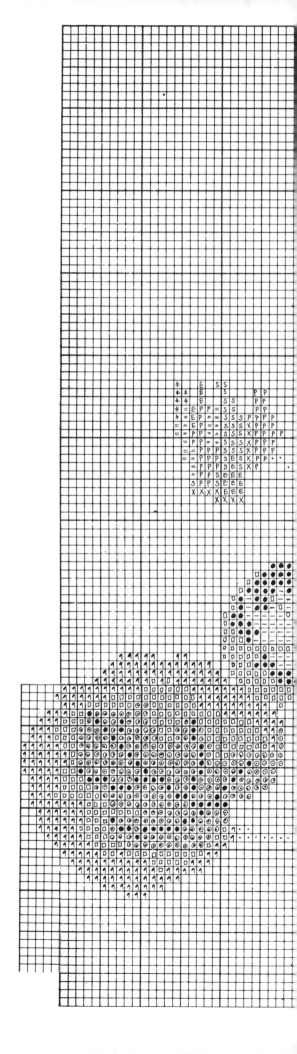

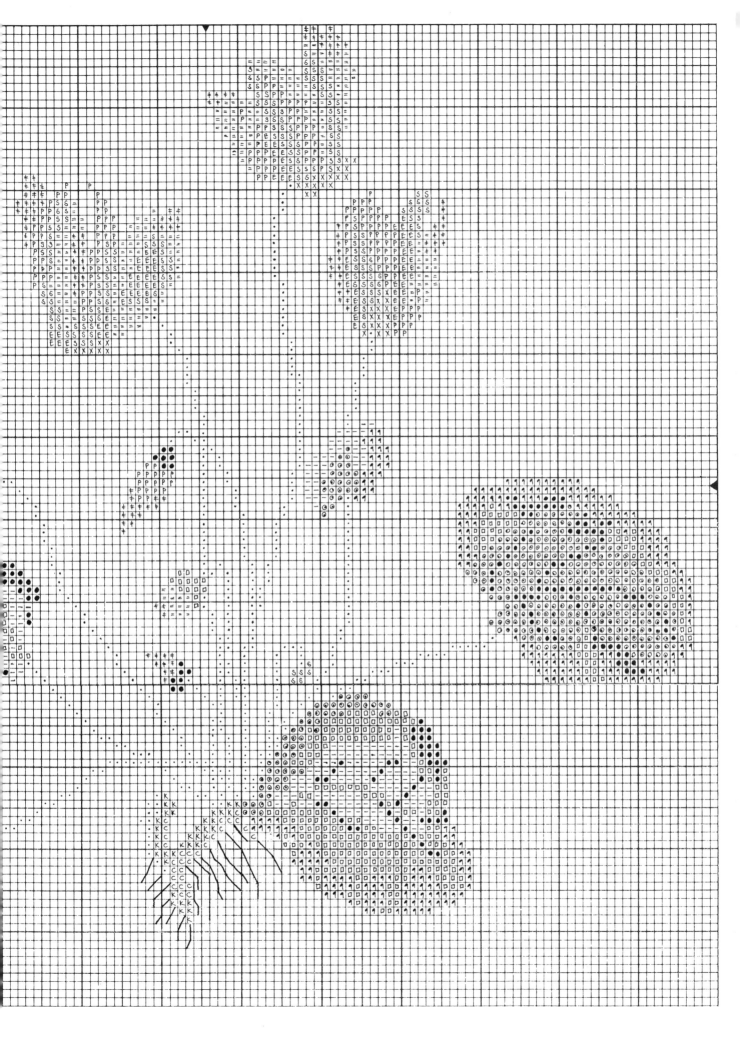

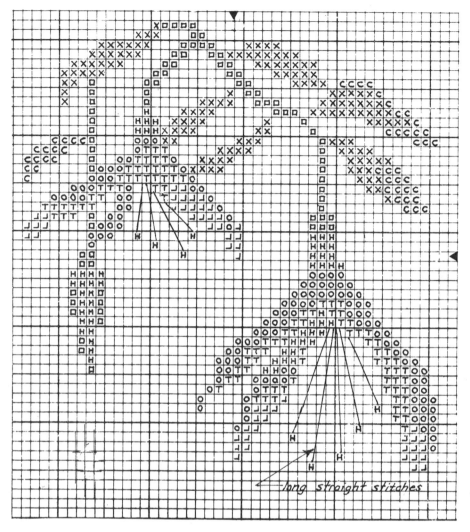

Fuchsia

Stitch count 45×47

The Maori name for the Fuchsia is Kotukutuku. There are hundreds of varieties which are found throughout New Zealand. The sample is worked in pinks on cream Jobelan but the colours can be changed quite easily by choosing four colours ranging from dark to light.

The long stamens are best worked in one long straight thread of the deepest colour and this is done on completion of the rest of the cross-stitch.

long straight stitches

Colour chart for Fuchsia

DMC	Symbol	Anchor	Colour
3685	H	072	Maroon
3687	O	070	Deep pink
3688	T	069	Med pink
3689	⌐	068	Light pink
367	X	245	Green
320	C	243	Med green
906	□	256	Bright green

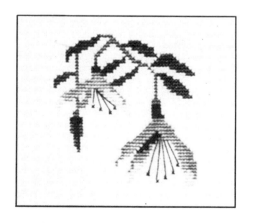

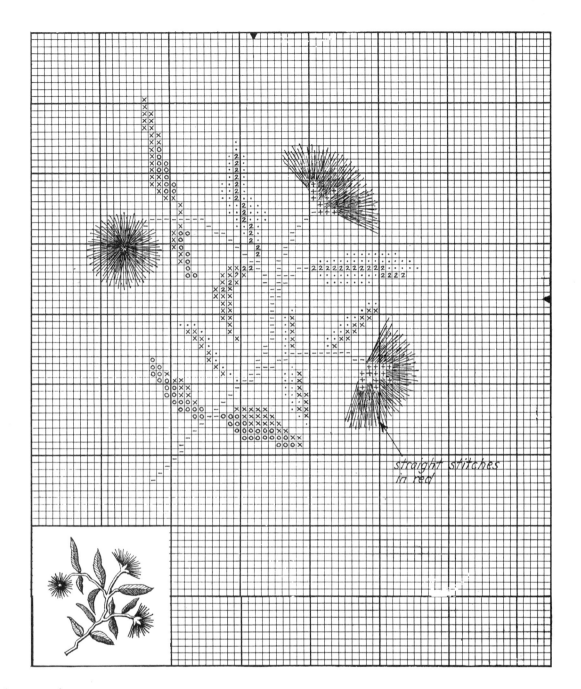

straight stitches in red

Pohutukawa

Stitch count 47×55

The sample is worked on cream Jobelan. The design is most attractive as a small picture or, worked on a coarser material, on a cushion. The stamens are worked in long straight stitches. The easiest way to do these is to put in a few stitches spaced at regular intervals and then fill in the remainder; this gives you an even-looking flower.

The pohutakawa is a truly noble tree in or out of flower. It is a tree of northern coastal places growing on cliffs above the sea and fringing beaches and lakes. Because it is a blaze of colour when in flower about the middle of December it is often referred to as the New Zealand Christmas tree.

Colour chart for Pohutukawa

DMC	Symbol	Anchor	Colour
3052	X	860	Med green
3053	O	858	Light green
839	–	905	Slate brown
927	+	848	Light silver
3051	•	862	Dark green
936	Z	846	Olive green
45		815	Dark red

Flower — straight stitches

New Zealand Pigeon

Stitch count 119×100

This species of pigeon has the Maori names Kuku and Kereru. It is undoubtedly the finest for both its brilliant plumage and its size.

It is widely distributed throughout New Zealand in bush areas. The pigeon feeds on the leaves of many shrubs and the fruits of native trees. The colour of pigeons varies from area to area.

In this pigeon design I have taken the mountain lines out to the edge of the mounting in the frame. The lines can be extended or shortened according to the frame. The mountains are worked in 1 thread, as is the tree in the background. This gives a better feeling of distance. The eye is back stitched in black and then half of it is over back stitched in white. The end of the beak has one half cross-stitch. The model is worked on cream Jobelan.

Colour chart for Pigeon

DMC	Symbol	Mez	Colour
520	X	862	Dark green
522	–	860	Med green
524	O	858	Light green
610	V	833	Med brown
611	Z	832	Med light brown
612	/	831	Light brown
Black	■	Black	
White	•	White	
986	□	245	Bright green
902	●	72	Maroon
221	|	896	Med pink
315	‡	897	Dark pink
223	S	895	Light pink
3021	H	905	Earth brown
318	†	398	Med grey
415	=	397	Light grey

Back Stitching — Mountain: 862. Eye: White. Beak: 905.

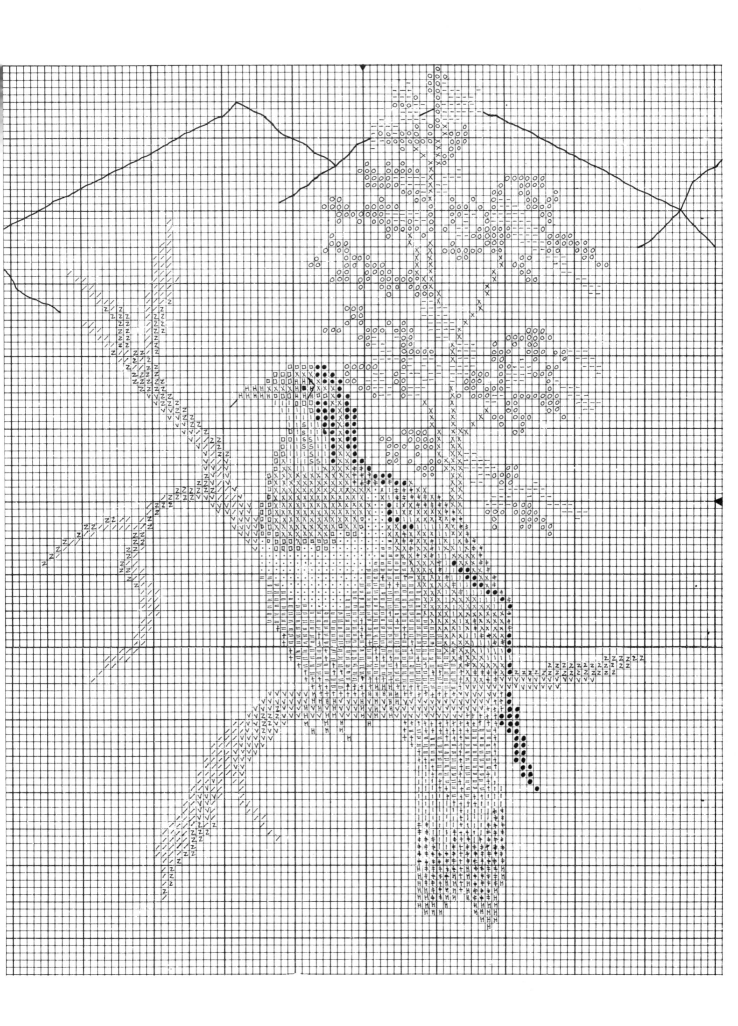

Adelie Penguin

Stitch count 52×50

The model is worked on grey Jobelan and this sets off the white in the penguin. This is an easy bird to cross-stitch as there are not many colours in the design, therefore it is quick to do.

The white of the eye has black back stitching around it in a diamond shape. The webbed feet and the beak are also back stitched in black.

The Adelie penguin is found from Campbell Island down to the Antarctic.

Colour chart for Penguin			
DMC	Symbol	Anchor	Colour
Black	\	Black	
White	⦂	White	
918	7	341	Red brown
318	□	398	Med grey

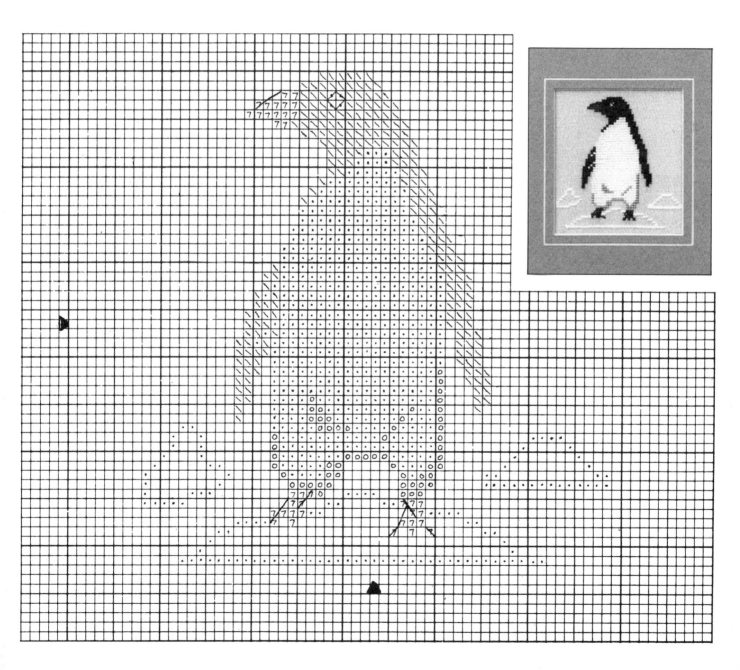

Colour chart for White Heron

DMC	Symbol	Anchor	Colour
White	:		White
928	□	847	Dull blue
927	\	848	Light dull blue
317	+	400	Dark grey
799	7	130	Sea blue
3021	=	905	Earth brown
640	C	903	Light earth brown
Black	U	Black	
676	<	311	Light orange

White Heron

Stitch count 46×44

The model of the white heron is worked on grey Jobelan but is most attractive worked on a pale blue or green. It makes an attractive pair with the penguin. The back stitching on the beak is worked in the light gold shade.

The white heron nests around the Okarito Lagoon in Westland but is often found during the winter months around coastal harbours of the North Island.

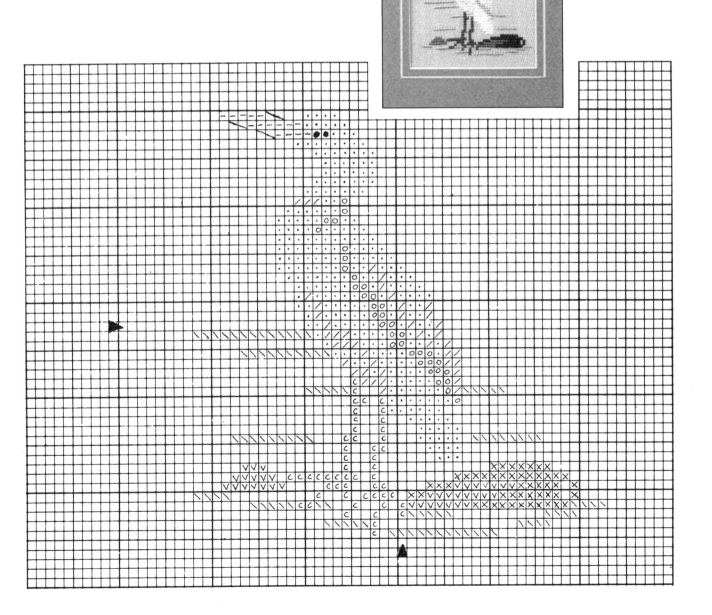

Pukeko

Stitch count 78×67

In New Zealand this bird is commonly known only by its Maori name Pukeko. It is found near water, e.g., swamps, lakes, lagoons, etc. It is a very reluctant flyer but a very fast runner. Though native to New Zealand it is also found in Australia where it is known as the swamp hen.

The back stitching is marked on the chart. I find it is usually preferable to use 1 strand of cotton on a fine material for back stitching. This does not make the back stitching look quite so heavy.

Colour chart for Pukeko

DMC	Symbol	Mez	Colour
Black	■	Black	
White	•	White	
823	×	127	Navy blue
796	\	134	Bright blue
797	‖	133	Med bright blue
3371	O	382	Dark brown
898	H	359	Brown
420	6	375	Tan brown
355	e	341	Red brown
500	Z	879	Dark green
501			878	Med green
809	–	130	Med blue
3345	L	269	Dark green
3347	●	267	Med green
3348	+	265	Light green

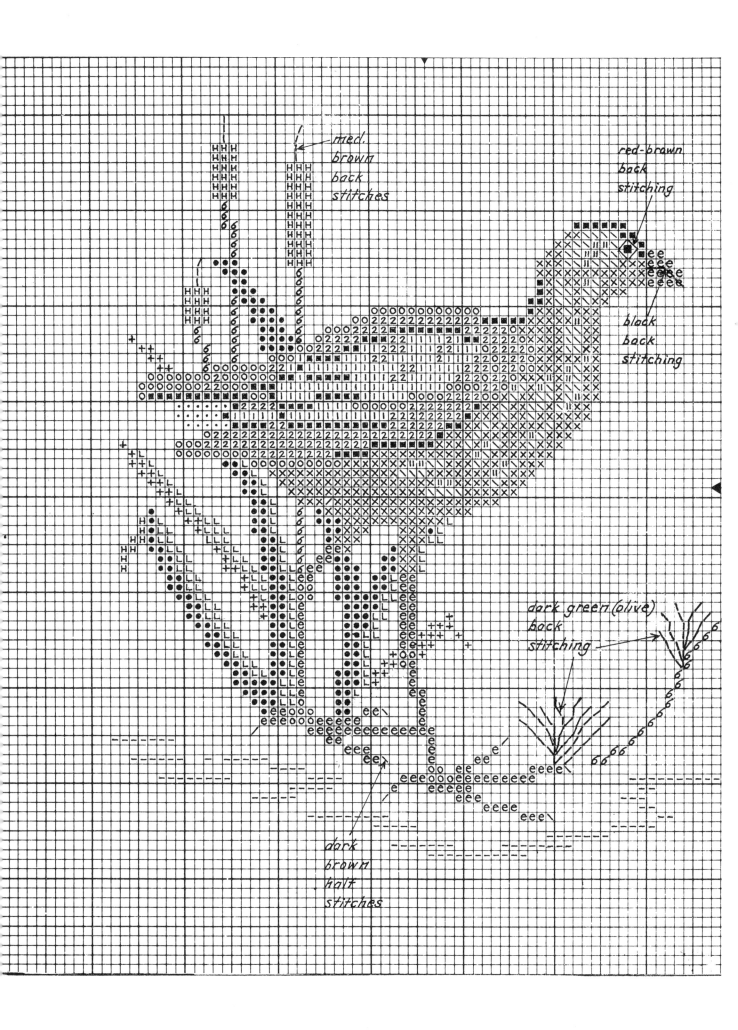

Keas

Stitch count 120×107

This bird is also known as the alpine parrot. It feeds almost entirely on alpine vegetation. The kea is found in the South Island high country but often migrates to the lowlands of Westland during winter. This cheeky bird builds its nest in rocky crevices or hollow logs.

Its colouring is most unusual, so it makes a most attractive picture for embroidery. The mountains are worked in back stitch using 1 thread of the medium grey. There is 1 stitch of back stitch at the end of the beak on each bird.

Colour chart for Keas

DMC	Symbol	Mez	Colour
3046	‡	887	Light curry brown
3045	–	888	Med curry brown
610	□	889	Dark curry brown
3021	×	905	Earth brown
640	●	903	Light earth brown
3051	E	845	Dark yellow green
3011	S	844	Med yellow green
3012	P	843	Light yellow green
3013	=	842	Lightest yellow green
733	C	280	Lime green
Black	■	Black	
White	•	White	
648	H	900	Lightest grey
3022	O	8581	Light grey
646	V	399	Med grey
844	/	400	Dark grey
612			854	Green brown
3047	+	852	Light green brown
938	¶	381	Dark brown

Back stitching in eyes 887/3046. Half stitch on beak 905/3021. Mountains 8581/3022.

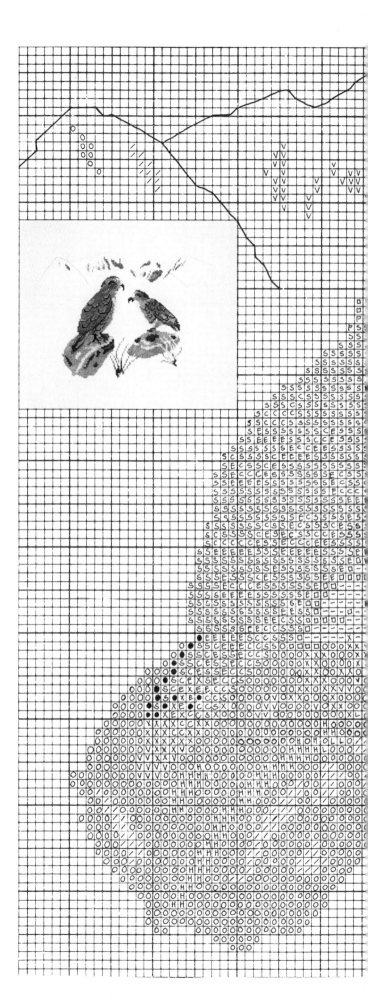

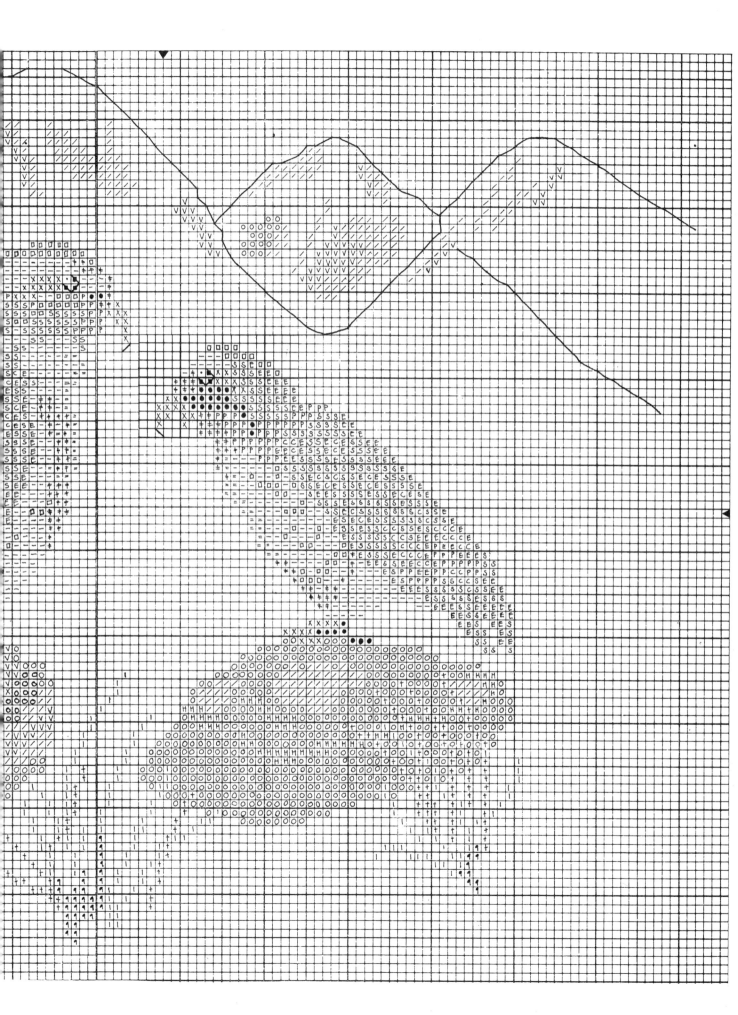

Pied Stilt

Stitch count 139×87

This bird is widely distributed throughout New Zealand. It is fairly distinct with its long red/brown legs and black-and-white plumage. The pied stilt is a familiar sight on shallow harbours throughout the country and nests in sand dunes and on boulder banks.

The water around the small bird is worked in 1 strand of thread and the water around the bigger bird is worked in 2 strands. The beak on both birds is finished off in a straight stitch to give length to the beak. The model is worked on light taupe Jobelan but is most attractive on a grey or fawn background.

Colour chart for Pied Stilts

DMC	Symbol	Mez	Colour
Black	X	Black	
White	•	White	
415	V	397	Light grey
318	O	398	Med grey
413	=	401	Dark grey
500	Z	879	Dark green
501			878	Med green
932	●	977	Med blue
931	‡	976	Med light blue
918	■	341	Red brown
920	C	339	Light red brown
3021	/	905	Earth brown
640	–	903	Med earth brown
370	+	856	Green brown
372	□	854	Med green brown
3047	S	852	Light green brown

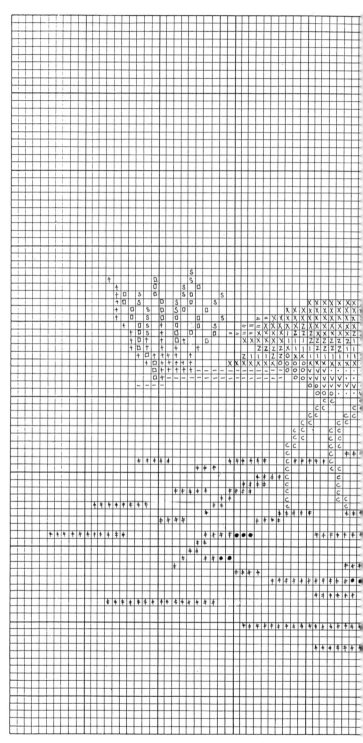

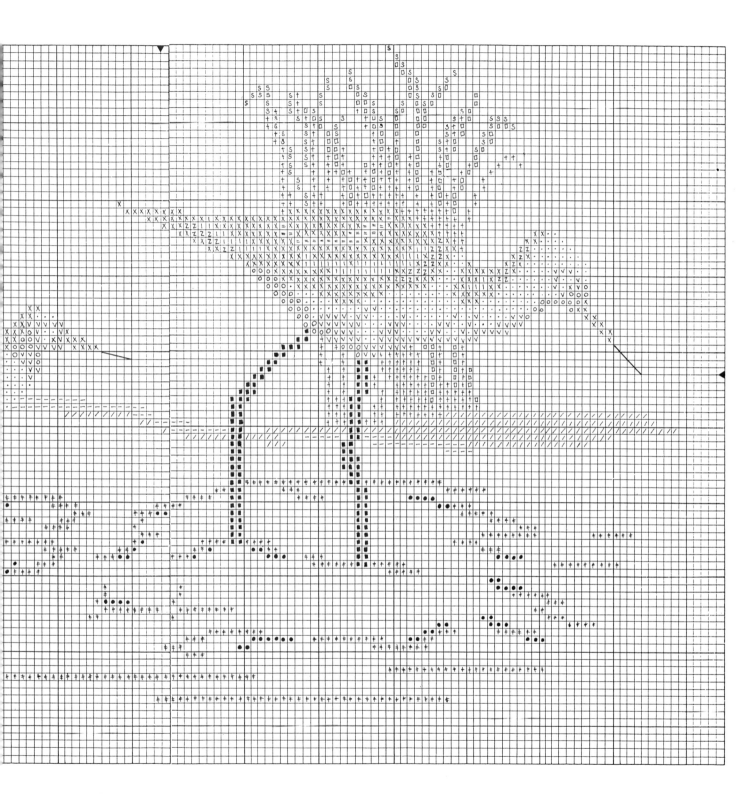

Saddleback

Stitch count 77×69

The Maori name for the saddleback is Teike. This bird is about the same size as a tui. The colours vary between the North and South Islands, but in both cases there are reddish brown markings across the back. Saddlebacks have been under threat of extinction and now are mainly confined to the northern offshore islands of the North Island.

The back stitch is worked in 1 thread according to the colours stated on the chart.

Colour chart for Saddleback

DMC	Symbol	Mez	Colour
Black	■	Black	
White	•	White	
500	O	879	Dark green
501	⅄	878	Med green
501	X	877	Med light green
355	N	341	Dark red brown
919	)	340	Red brown
356	))	339	Med red brown
758	\	338	Light red brown
3371			382	Dark brown
413	–	401	Dark grey
608	:	335	Scarlet
580	↑	281	Yellow green
581	∧	280	Light yellow green
350	◗	013	Light red
352	⌿	011	Med red pink
420	➤	375	Light brown
318	Z	398	Med grey
801	V	359	Med brown

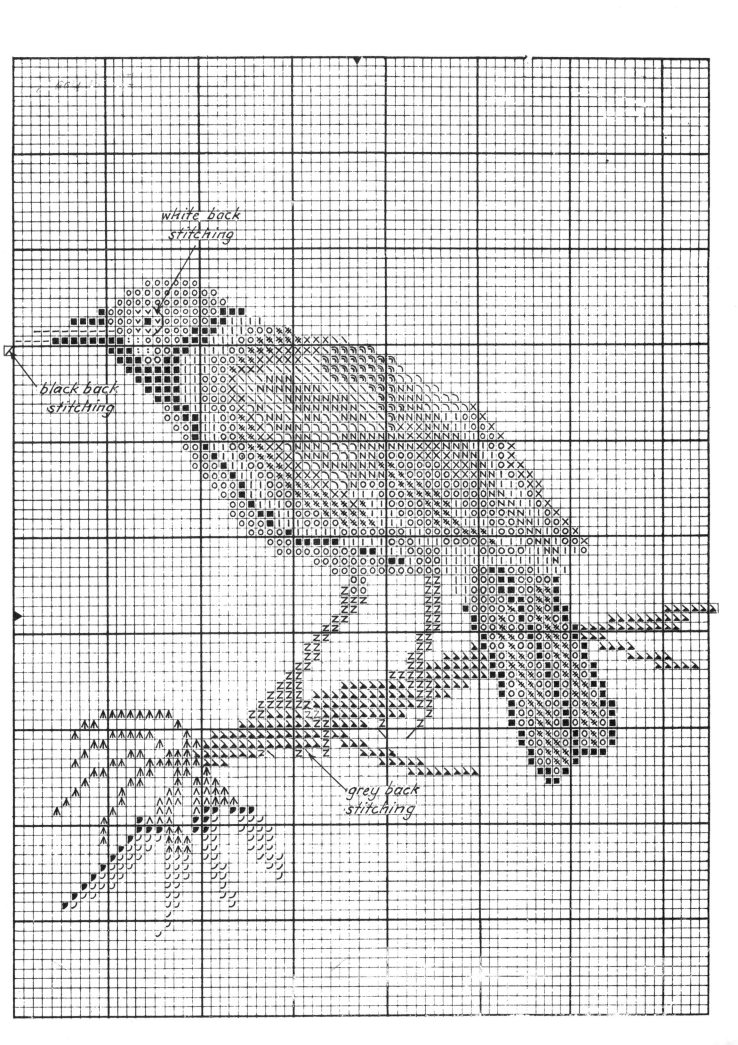

white back
stitching

black back
stitching

grey back
stitching

Kiwi, Grey Warbler and Morepork

These 3 birds make delightful small pictures and can be framed or used on boxes or the covers of books. They are very useful designs to have in one's collection.

The kiwi is probably the best known bird in New Zealand but the grey warbler has by far the most beautiful voice. It is a very small bird and camouflages very well into most surroundings. The morepork is generally seen only at night when it is hunting.

The stitch sizes of the warbler and kiwi are approximately 42×33 and the morepork is 51×43. The back stitching is all worked in one thread according to the colours marked on the chart.

All models are worked on Jobelan 28 threads per inch (12 threads per centimetre). The size of material required is 15×50 centimetres for all 4 birds. Always allow at least 15 centimetres outside design area. Suggested material is cream Jobelan, fine or coarse.

Colour chart for Kiwi, Grey Warbler and Morepork

DMC	Symbol	Mez	Colour
Black	■	Black	
White	•	White	
413	×	401	Dark grey
318	ω	398	Med grey
762	●	397	Light grey
3371	⁒	382	Dark brown
801	‖	380	Med dark brown
433	C	359	Med brown
434	L	357	Light brown
3021	–	905	Earth brown
640	Z	903	Light earth brown
869	6	375	Tan brown
3078	O	300	Cream
822	✳	390	Fawn
307	BS	290	Bright yellow
937	∩	269	Dark green
470			267	Med green
606	▲	046	Bright red
831	V	889	Curry brown

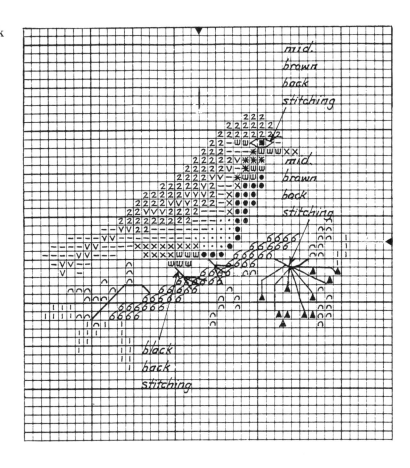

mid.
brown
back
stitching

mid.
brown
back
stitching

black
back
stitching

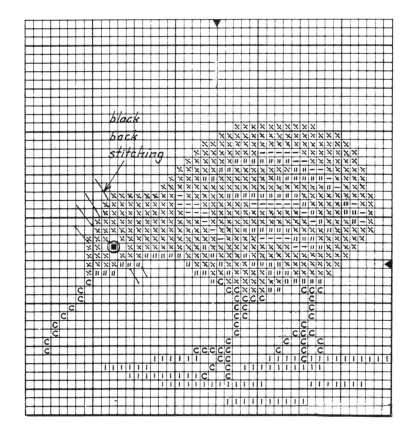

black
back
stitching

Colour chart for Lacebark and Harebell

DMC	Symbol	Mez	Colour
935	–	269	Dark green
469	¶	267	Med green
3348	□	265	Light green
471	●	254	Bright green
3021	×	905	Earth brown
White	•	White	
727	K	295	Light yellow
3047	W	853	Light tan
554	©	119	Light mauve
820	L	134	Dark blue
798	Y	131	Med blue
799	§	130	Med light blue
800	■	129	Light blue

Harebell and lacebark

Stitch count approximately 96×28

Both samples are worked on cream Jobelan. The back stitching on the lacebark is 845/612 and the stamens are 905/3021. I suggest one thread to be used for the back stitching.

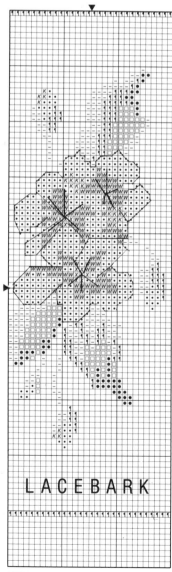

HAREBELL

LACEBARK